"The noblest art is that of making others happy"
P.T Barnum

This is a work of fiction. Names, characters, businesses, places, events, locales, and incidents either are the products of the author's imagination or used in a fictitious manner. Any resemblance to actual persons, living or dead, or actual events is purely coincidental.

Text copyright © 2022 by Robert Wilson

Illustrations copyright © by Robert Wilson

No part of this publication may be reproduced, stored in a retrieval system, or transmitted in any form or by any means, electronic, mechanical, photocopying, recording, or otherwise, without prior written permission from the author.

First paperback edition in this format 2022

ISBN 979-84-4716-611-3 (paperback)

Learn more about Robert Wilson on Instagram at

@jiujitsuandme

"Sasha, it's time to go!" dad called from downstairs.

"Coming!" Sasha replied with excitement.

Sasha was on her way to her first jiu-jitsu lesson. A jiu-jitsu instructor had come to her school last week and demonstrated some techniques for the students. Sasha was delighted that her dad agreed to take her to the local academy.

As Sasha was entering the jiu-jitsu academy for the first time, she saw a clean matted floor with children wearing white uniforms and different coloured belts. There were ten children in her lesson. Sasha was happy to see a couple of girls in her lesson, as she feared she may be the only one. She took off her shoes and joined the children on the mat.

Sasha really enjoyed her first lesson. At the beginning, they played games that she knew from school. Then Coach Lewis showed them some basic framing techniques. Sasha was then paired with one of the other girls at the end of the lesson to work on the techniques.

Sasha began training three times a week. She worked very hard and always listened to the coach's instructions. Coach Lewis was good at explaining how and when a move should be performed.

One day, after a jiu-jitsu lesson, Sasha sat on the mat with her face in her hands.
"What's the matter?" asked Coach Lewis.
"I can't seem to get the techniques to work on the boys in sparring," Sasha sobbed.
"Sasha, the boys are training longer than you," Coach Lewis said. "They know the techniques you know and how to counter them. Just keep showing up and make sure to ask lots of questions. You also need to do one more thing!"
Sasha looked up from the mat.
"You need to have fun! You need to enjoy your time on the mat. We all have good days and bad days. Once you are having fun, training regularly, and asking questions, then the boys here are in big trouble!" Coach Lewis said with a smile.

Sasha made sure to have fun during every lesson. She participated in all the games and enjoyed drilling the techniques. What she loved the most about jiu-jitsu was the sparring at the end of the lesson. She just loved the competition.

After several months of training, Sasha went to the martial arts shop to buy a new uniform, since the white one she was using was an old karate uniform she found in her closet. Sasha wanted

something that made her feel powerful. As she was browsing through the uniforms, she spotted a pink one. Her eyes opened wide with delight.

"Dad, I want this one!" she said while picking up the uniform.
"Why did you choose this one?" dad asked.
"You wouldn't understand," Sasha replied jokingly.

Sasha wanted to prove to herself that girls can be just as good as the boys, and with her new pink uniform, she was ready for the challenge. Sasha paid close attention every time the coach demonstrated a technique. She always asked to be paired with a boy when training. The boys in the academy were very good to the girls, they would resist just enough to help her use her frames properly, to remain safe and to practice the techniques.

If a technique was not working, Sasha would ask the coach questions. She discovered that one little adjustment to a technique can make a big difference.

Sasha realised that playing full guard allowed her to control the boys better. Her full guard frustrated the boys as it limited their movement. Full guard became her favourite position.

In one lesson, Sasha had a boy in her full guard. The boy gripped her collar, so Sasha grabbed his sleeve. She then shifted her hips slightly to the side, grabbed the boy's pants at the knee with her other hand

and swept the boy over into full mount. It was the first time Sasha swept a boy in sparring; she was ecstatic.

Upon leaving the academy one evening, Sasha saw a poster for a mini jiu-jitsu tournament on the notice board. She wanted to compete and test her jiu-jitsu against other girls, as there weren't too many in her academy.

Sasha put her name on the registration paper. She felt nervous, but she knew that she had to face her fears head on.

After a month of training and focus, the day of the tournament arrived. Sasha was warming-up when she heard the referee call her name. She walked over to the mats and looked across at her opponent. To her surprise, it was a boy.

Sasha couldn't believe it, she thought she would be matched against a girl, but no other girls signed up to compete. "Sasha, you have been training for ten months now," Coach Lewis said. "You have a stripe on your white belt. You do very well against the other boys in the academy. Your advantage here is that this boy will underestimate you. Have fun!"

Sasha tied her hair in a ponytail, took a deep breath and walked confidently onto the mat. She shook the referee's hand and her opponent's hand. The match began.

Sasha immediately got grips on the boy's collar and sleeve. The boy was a lot stronger than her, but Sasha knew it was to be expected. The boy took Sasha to the ground with a foot sweep. Sasha managed to use her arms as frames to stop the boy from getting side control. She then hip-escaped and got the boy in her full guard.

While in full guard, Sasha adjusted to a deeper collar grip and made sure the boy could not posture up. She felt calm and in control.
The boy was trying very hard to posture up and to break her collar grip.

Sasha prevented this by bringing her knees close to her chest. Sasha then gripped the sleeve as well as the collar, opened her legs, and attempted a scissor sweep.
The boy was so focused on breaking Sasha's grips, that Sasha swept him easily and got into full mount.

The boy scrambled on bottom. Sasha remained calm and adjusted her hips when the boy moved to the side. Sasha couldn't believe that the boy exposed his back. Sasha got a seatbelt grip and executed a back-take. The boy lifted his chin. Sasha seized the opportunity and went for a choke and squeezed. The boy tapped Sasha on the arm, ending the match.

Sasha won the match by submission; she couldn't believe it. It was the first time she submitted a boy in jiu-jitsu. She was so proud of herself for not giving up and proved to herself that girls can do anything with self-belief, hard work and determination.

The End

Printed in Great Britain
by Amazon